PASSINGS

PRAISE FOR *PASSINGS*

In poems at once heartbreaking and illuminating, Holly Hughes gives extinction a very personal face. She makes it clear that the bell tolls not only for the fifteen species she elegizes, but for us as well. Her words prompt us to love and revere the beauty and music of the birds still left, and to remember their well-being in all the choices we make.

—Lorraine Anderson
editor of *Earth & Eros: A Celebration in Words & Photographs*

"No one knows for sure you're gone," Holly Hughes writes of the Eskimo curlew. Most of its fellows on this ex-life list, *rarae aves* no longer, are *aves extincta*. But they've not gone from the scene without grace. Even their names are poems—O'o, dodo, great auk, Spix's macaw—and names, thanks to *Passings*, that will remain on the wing as long as there are lips to say them.

—Robert Michael Pyle
author of *Evolution of the Genus Iris: Poems*

This is a heartbreaking and illuminating memorial to all the birds that we have lost, a painful memorial in an era of extinctions, climate change, and destruction of the Amazon rainforest that asks us to think about which birds we're losing in our own backyards, our own neighborhoods.

—Ginny Lim
Before Columbus Foundation Board Member
American Book Awards Ceremony, October 22, 2017

I can't say enough good things about Holly J. Hughes's beautiful chapbook *Passings*. Each of its fifteen poems mourns the extinction of a bird, some familiar like the dodo and ivory-billed woodpecker, others unknown to me—'til now—including the elephant bird and paradise parrot. In a curious way, Hughes brings these lost creatures back to life through the precision of her language and the vivid evocations only poetry can deliver. The birds live, at least, on the page, if not on earth. I found myself all the more deeply moved for their absence from the world. That absence, of course, is in no small part—maybe entirely so—due to human activity, including climate disruption, whether for the demand for colorful feathers for women's hats or for food or because of the eradication of habitats. There's a sobering lesson in these sad brief poems. History, ornithology, poetry—it's all here. To all my birder friends out there, order this book now. Ditto if you're a non-birder.

—Ed Harkness
author of *The Law of the Unforeseen*

The poems reflect Pound's dictum about the luminous detail—just the pith and gist—so there's just enough information, but not too much. The reader gets these flashes of imagery. At the end of each poem, after getting to know the bird, when the bird is gone, we feel it. It's really gone.

—Mike Dillon
"A Quiet Letter to the World: An Interview with Holly J. Hughes"
Rain Taxi, Fall 2016 print edition

PASSINGS

Holly J. Hughes

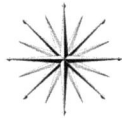

Wandering Aengus Press
Eastsound, WA

Library of Congress Cataloguing-in-Publication Data available.

Second Edition

Winner of the 2017 American Book Award

Poetry
ISBN: 978-0-578-46329-2

Printed in the United States of America

Cover Image: "Passenger Pigeons in Flight" by Lewis Cross, 1937.

Feather Image Design: Myrna Keliher, Expedition Press.

Author Photo: Diane Haugsvar

Wandering Aengus Press is dedicated to publishing works to enrich lives and make the world a better place.

Wandering Aengus Press
PO Box 334 Eastsound, WA 98245
wanderingaenguspress.com

In memory of Eva Saulitis

1963 – 2016

CONTENTS

PASSINGS

PREFACE

*Some things qualify as silence, but they wake us
like the disappearance of birdcall that kept us asleep
because we took it as dream-stitch.*

Katie Ford

An early memory: flash of scarlet against tall drifts of snow. A cardinal swoops to the feeder outside our kitchen window. That's how I learned the color red, and from then on I associated red with that cardinal, which seemed a friend as it showed up each morning for its oily, black sunflower seeds that my father provided, no matter how deep the drifts.

When I look back on my life, I see that birds have always been part of my family, speaking to me, sometimes directly, sometimes indirectly. I remember waddling behind a flock of mallard ducks soon after learning to walk, intent on joining them. Later, while at summer camp in northern Minnesota, I recall an encounter with a great blue heron on a lake at dusk. The heron balances, motionless, on one leg in the tall reeds as the setting sun suffuses the sky, the heron's ball-bearing eye peering into my own. Loons began calling to me, their wild laugh beckoning me north and west, and I followed, finding myself fishing in Alaska with a whole raft of seabirds to meet: horned and tufted puffins, ancient murrelets, whiskered auklets, and pigeon guillemots. I soon came to recognize them as new members of my family: the smooth, white breast of the common murre perched on rocky ledges, the orange legs of the black oystercatcher pacing the shoreline, the quick, nervous dive of the phalarope. When the *Exxon Valdez* fetched up on Bligh Reef in 1989, I left my job writing catalog copy and flew to Seward to work on the spill. I was given a job running the medic boat and picking up oiled seabirds to take to the rehabilitation center in Seward. As we scooped up each oiled, limp bird in a net, each dying seabird felt like a pending death among my own kin.

These days, the birds in my life are fewer but still distinct: Cormorants hanging their wings out to dry as I wait for the ferry to take me to work each morning, the kingfisher perched on the telephone line above the slough as I drive home each afternoon, the osprey that follows me up the beach, the pileated woodpecker that drums the stump outside my writing studio, the lilting call of the Swainson's thrush on evening walks. I can't imagine my life without birds, even if their presence is fleeting. They are my family, my relations; without them, my world would be a less vibrant, less musical place.

As with that first scarlet flash of the cardinal, birds bring me into the present, remind me of the necessity of beauty, of song. Birds punctuate our days, our lives, whether the call of a solitary meadowlark at the edge of a clearing or the raucous cacophony of a kittiwake rookery on the Alaskan coast.

Like birds, poems are fleeting, flitting through our consciousness before they come to roost in our hearts. Perhaps it was inevitable that poetry and birds would come together for me. This series began more than a decade ago, fittingly, with Audubon's iconic painting of the passenger pigeon. Decades earlier, I'd found a print in a used bookstore in Sitka, Alaska, and was haunted by it, returning several times to look at it and finally buy it. It stayed rolled up in the closet for years, until one day I unrolled, matted and framed it, and hung it on the wall of my cabin. Of course, I knew the story of Martha, the last passenger pigeon, who died in the Cincinnati Zoo in 1914. The next morning, when I woke, the birds in the print seemed to call for a poem, so I wrote about them. I wanted them to have company, so I began writing about other extinct birds, finding out, sadly, there was no shortage of choices. As I read more, I grew dispirited by the statistics on the numbers of extinct birds and set the project aside.

Then I happened upon a book, *Swift as a Shadow: Extinct and Endangered Birds*; its powerful photographs by Rosamond Purcell provided the visual inspiration I needed to return to this project. Seeing her poignant, moving images, I was inspired to add my voice of witness as a poet to these birds' passings in hope that these poems might serve as both elegy and warning.

As I wrote these poems, I intuitively shaped them into couplets. It seemed fitting to use a traditional form to honor birds' ancient presence in literature. Only later did I see that the form on the page might also suggest wings. As I put this chapbook together, this form seemed apt, perhaps suggesting that the lives of birds and humans are forever coupled. In 2017, reports released by the National Audubon Society chronicling the effect of climate change on bird populations warned that many species of birds are already adjusting their range as their habitat changes. Like the canary in the coal mine, birds are letting us know what's ahead for all of us. We're in this together.

I'll leave it to the scientists to count, chronicle, and calculate cause and consequences. Poems serve another purpose. As Christopher Cokinos points out in his moving book, *Hope Is the Thing with Feathers*, "Knowing whatever we can about these vanished birds restores them…to a habitat we still can save: our moral imagination."

Take note. These birds are still singing to us. We must listen.

Holly J. Hughes
Indianola WA

You could not see a cloud, because
No cloud was in the sky:
No birds were flying overhead —
There were no birds to fly.

Lewis Carroll

Through the Looking Glass

Passenger Pigeon

Echtopistes migratorius

> *from the painting by James J. Audubon, 1824. On Sept. 1, 1914,*
> *Martha, the last passenger pigeon died in the Cincinnati Zoo.*

See how she bends to him, her beak held within his
while she waits for his food to rise up to her hunger.

He rests on the arcing branch, his neck a perfect answer to hers,
wings held aloft and slightly splayed while long tail feathers stream

away, Prussian blue going to dusk, breast russet, branch below
studded with viridian lichen to match his coat, colors chosen

by Audubon as he painted them in courtship *in situ*.
See how her colors foreshadow the fall — dun, mustard, black—

how her tail balances his wings painted in parallel planes,
how the drooping oak leaf holds them in place, stasis

in which they are aware of no one but each other.
Audubon captured them in gouache, graphite, and pastels,

not knowing they would soon be gone; in his time
they were more numerous than all other species combined.

They say the pigeons flew over the banks of the Ohio River
for three days in succession, sounding *like a hard gale at sea.*

Years later, guns splattered shot into skies stormy with pigeons.
Thousands plummeted, filling railroad cars bound for fine restaurants.

Now, of those hundreds of millions that once darkened
the skies, we are left with Martha, who never lived in the wild,

stuffed in the Smithsonian, Prussian blue feathers stiff,
glass eyes staring, waiting, still, for her mate.

PASSINGS

GREAT AUK

Pinguinus impennis

Once, flocks of great auks nested on the rocks
off the coast of the North Atlantic. The first bird

to be called a penguin, they were built to swim,
but slow, defenseless on land. Pairs mated for life,

nesting shoulder to shoulder in dense rookeries,
laying one egg on bare rock, taking turns tending

the egg until it hatched. Devoted parents, they cared
for their young even after they'd fledged;

adults were seen swimming, chicks perched
on their backs. In those days, a sighting of great auks

quickened a sailor's heart, signaled landfall ahead.
Their end came when the Europeans love for featherbeds

brought hunters in search of down (after every eider
had been plucked, gone). To loosen their plumage,

auks were boiled in cauldrons over fires fed with the oil
of auks killed before them, since there was little wood to be found.

In 1830, a volcano erupted off the tip of Iceland submerging
the last nesting colony on *Geirfuglasker*, great auk rock.

Refugees, the auks moved to the island of Eldey. There,
on July 3, 1844, the last pair was killed by hunters

gathering specimens for a museum. Here's how one hunter
described the scene: *I took him by the neck, he flapped his wings.*

He made no cry. I strangled him.

PASSINGS

LABRADOR DUCK

Camptorhynchus labradorius

Your black-and-white plumage earned you many names:
Skunk Duck, Pied Duck, and worst of all, Fool Duck.

To you, the distinction of being the first species
among endemic North American birds to go extinct.

Ornithologists can't say exactly why, since you,
unlike some birds, could fly. Perhaps your diet

of mollusks, shoveled and sifted in the shallows
by your unique beak; perhaps your eggs

were too easy to harvest; perhaps your trusting
nature made you an easy mark for hunters; perhaps

because your flesh rotted quickly in the open air
markets of Baltimore, mindless revenge

on a creature deemed useless. But when you flew,
your wings whistled, whistled as you tried to escape

a pound of double B fired from the ducking sloops
killing or wounding hundreds at a shot.

Your numbers dropped; no one believed you,
so numerous, could be wiped out. One by one,

you took your leave until a December day in 1878
in the lowlands outside Elmira, New York,

a young lad shot a black-and-white duck, packed it
home to his hungry family, who were grateful to eat,

who could not know they were eating the last Labrador duck.

PASSINGS

CAROLINA PARAKEET

Conuropsis carolinensis

> *Incas, the last Carolina parakeet, died in his cage*
> *at the Cincinnati Zoo on Feb. 21, 1918, only six months*
> *after the death of Lady Jane, his companion of thirty-two years.*

From Mexico to New York they flew, tail feathers streaming,
startling in the monochrome of winter's eastern shore.

When their forests were cut, they swooped to the farmlands
in waves of color — yellow, green, orange — lit in fruit trees,

found the soft squish of peaches, cherries, figs. Descended
three hundred at a time, in crayon-box flocks, they were shot

by farmers defending their crops — who could fault them?
Shot for their tail feathers, all the rage on ladies' hats,

shot because they would not desert each other, each staying
by its wounded mate until hunters picked them off,

one by each last, bright, exotic, faithful one.

Heath Hen

Tympanuchus cupido cupido

Could be the heath hen was the main course when settlers
sat down to that first Thanksgiving dinner. From Maine

to Virginia, they were so plentiful that servants asked not
to be fed them more than three times a week. So plentiful

their flocks could never be depleted, settlers thought. Instead,
heath hens were one of the first bird species Americans tried

to save, passing a law in 1791 to protect them. By 1830,
the heath hen's decline gained the notice of Audubon,

but still their numbers dropped. By the 1870s, they survived
only on Martha's Vineyard, displaying for their mates. When fifty

remained, a hunting ban was imposed, a sanctuary established.
Those protected birds grew to 2,000, then a fire wiped out

their breeding habitat. That winter, goshawks reduced the flock,
and those left fell victim to a disease spread by domestic turkeys.

By 1927, only thirteen heath hens — all but two males — still
boomed for a mate's affection. On March 11, 1932, the last

survivor, Booming Ben, was believed seen, but not again.
His remains were never found.

PASSINGS

Eskimo Curlew

Numenius Borealis

I grew up reading *The Last of the Curlews* before bed,
your crescent-moon beak beckoning me north.

Even then you were almost gone, though millions of you
once filled the skies, migrating from the northern tundra

to South America, feeding on grasshoppers along the way.
Within twenty years, your vast flocks were brought down

by market hunters, fire suppression, tilling of the prairies,
eradication of grasshoppers. Before hunting was banned,

two million curlews were killed each year.
Here's the part that still makes me weep:

you were wiped out because you stayed
by your fallen companion; from you

I learned what loyalty means. Today, birders
search for you along Galveston's shore,

sometimes catch a glimpse, memory being so strong.
No one knows for sure you're gone. You live on

in the pages of a book, a waning crescent moon.

PASSINGS

Hawaiian O'o

Moho nobilis

Considered royal, their brilliant plumage once adorned the robes
of Hawaiian kings. Large and confident, the O'o were trapped,

choice yellow feathers plucked from tufts beneath
their wings, woven into sacred robes, then released

back to the wild. If not released, they were eaten: *a great delicacy
when fried in their own fat*, native Hawaiians reported.

Though their feathers had been plucked for generations,
they were still plentiful when Captain Cook landed.

The Europeans brought avian diseases, cleared
the land, collected them as song birds.

In 1898 the musket arrived, and thousands fell
from the skies. The last Hawaiian O'o sighted

on the slopes of Mauna Loa was still singing,
still listening for its mate.

PASSINGS

DODO

Raphus cucullatus

O Dodo, how can so little be known about you, most maligned
of extinct birds? I encountered you first on the school playground

as an insult, looked you up in the *Encyclopedia Brittanica*
and found you in an artist's drawing based on reports from sailors,

looking fat and stupid even to me then, and already
you were extinct: *Gone the way of the dodo.*

Later I learned you were just a clumsy relative of pigeons
who'd lost your ability to fly; you had no predators

before European sailors arrived on the shores of Mauritius,
sailors who took your trusting nature as a sign of stupidity.

Cursed by evolution and the easy judgment of sailors,
you didn't even taste good: the Dutch called you "disgusting bird."

Still, you became a source of meat for passing sailors
but that's not what did you in. You laid only one egg,

your nest on the ground plundered by pigs, dogs, and monkeys
brought to the island by ship. Accounts tell us you were

once exhibited live on the streets of London. A curiosity.
What's curiouser still is this: a hundred years later,

you were gone. What remains are the bones of your head
and foot at Oxford, a few more bones scattered

across museums in Europe and Mauritius. Not
even drawings of you can be verified. We have

only this pejorative—*you dodo*—as proof that you once
walked the earth, doomed by your trusting nature,

your extinction a cautionary tale
(if we don't prove to be dodos ourselves).

PASSINGS

Elephant Bird

Aepyornis maximus

In 1658, the French governor of Madagascar described a giant bird
dwelling in the island's remote reaches. Over ten feet tall,

the bird weighed a thousand pounds and laid the biggest egg on record:
over a foot long and equal in volume to seven ostrich eggs,

180 chicken eggs or 12,000 hummingbird eggs, large enough
to feed a whole family, as it likely did. The elephant bird

may have inspired the legend of the *rukh*, which Sinbad
encounters in *The Thousand and One Nights*

and Marco Polo described as being strong enough
to seize an elephant with its talons. But its legendary might

couldn't save it; the few elephant birds that lived in isolated
valleys didn't last long, were believed gone by the end

of the seventeenth century. Four centuries later,
a single egg auctioned at Christie's in London

fetched more than a hundred thousand pounds.

PASSINGS

Rodriguez Solitaire

Pezophaps solitaria

They walk with such stately form and good grace
that one cannot help admiring and loving them.
                                        —Francois Leguat

In 1691, Leguat fled with fellow Huguenots
to the island of Rodriguez in the Indian Ocean.

There, enchanted with the flightless birds,
he drew them on the margins of his maps

like dragons drawn by sailors on ancient charts,
not knowing they too would become mythical.

The Huguenots praised the bird's delicious taste,
particularly when young and plump.

By the second half of the eighteenth century,
passing sailors in search of fresh meat

had hunted Leguat's beloved bird to naught.
When the solitaires were caught,

they made not a sound; they only shed tears.

PASSINGS

LAUGHING OWL

Sceloglaux albifacies

A hundred years ago, on dark nights, their laughter
echoed over the green fells of New Zealand.

Settlers say the haunting notes of their call
to each other came minutes before rain.

Languid during the day, the white-faced owls
were easy to capture. They fed on a native rat,

the kiore, whose extinction brought on their own.
In 1905, a settler told how a laughing owl could

always be coaxed from its hiding place in the rocks
after dusk by the squeeze and wheeze of an accordion.

He told how the owl would silently fly over, face
the music, listen   until the music ceased.

PASSINGS

Huia

Heteralocha acutirostris

The Maoris prized the huia for its white-tipped tail feathers
to wear in battle, give in friendship, wave during funeral rites.

Whenever the huia grew scarce, a Maori priest banned
their killing and the bird's population rebounded.

When Captain Cook landed on the shores
of New Zealand, European settlers ignored

the ban and the Maoris followed suit. Soon
the birds with the white-tipped tail feathers

grew scarce. Hunted, their habitat destroyed,
they fell victim to diseases brought by Europeans.

No more did the Maori wear their feathers.
The last sighting was in 1907. I want to believe

it was a Maori who caught the last glimpse.

Paradise Parrot

Psephotus pulcherrimus

No one can see the paradise parrot without
desiring to possess so beautiful and graceful
a bird but alas! one in a dozen survives a few
months and - dies suddenly in a fit.
                    —William Thomas Greene

Native to the grassy woodlands of eastern Australia,
paradise parrot lived in pairs, hollowing out its nest

in termite mounds, feeding on grass seeds.
Even by parrot standards, its plumage was colorful —

turquoise, aqua, scarlet — its tail stretched as long
as its body though it spent its time not in the air

but on the ground. Its numbers declined
after cattle arrived, depleting its grass seeds.

Sought after by bird collectors, it was captured
and exported, though few survived. By the end

of the nineteenth century, sightings were rare.
C.C. Jerrard photographed one of the last wild pairs:

"His whole body vibrated with the force and intensity
of his musical effort. It all seemed to indicate a very

intense little personality under the beautiful exterior."

PASSINGS

Spix's Macaw

Cyanopsitta spixii

1819: Johan Baptist von Spix sights a flash of blue wing.
The German naturalist explores northeast Bahia

and this little macaw he's not yet seen. He follows
the Rio São Francisco, nets the bird on the bank,

where it nests in the Caatinga forest, subsisting on seeds
and nuts of Caraiba and spurge, gives it his name.

In less than two centuries, his namesake will be gone
as Brazil is colonized, forests razed for farmland.

By 1998, the Spix's macaw dies out in the wild
except for one male. Conservationists release

a captive female hoping for one more chance
to save the wild population. Male parrots choose

their mates and she's accepted as a companion,
nothing more. Instead, his eye is on a female

of a different species, the Illiger's macaw.
When last seen, the wild male's blue wings

were flying off, flashing blue against hers of green.

PASSINGS

Ivory-Billed Woodpecker

Campephilus principalis

I wish I'd been at the sighting that inspired its nickname,
the Lord God bird. I'd love to see this woodpecker,

perhaps extinct, perhaps not; no one knows for sure.
Standing twenty inches tall with white wing patches

and a flashy red crest, who wouldn't say *Lord God,
look at that?* Once making its home in the hardwood

forests of the south, birders say its ivory bill could pierce
bark eight inches deep. Imagine the racket. Even so,

they were vulnerable: a single pair needed six square miles
of wet forest with dead trees in which to nest and search for grubs.

In 1948 when a Louisiana forest was cleared for a soy plantation,
the last population vanished. The Cuban subspecies survived

a few more decades, but by 1970, logging had reduced its population
to eight pairs. In the 1990s, explorers in the mountains near Moa

found fresh signs of feeding, caught a glimpse of a bird that may
have been the ivory bill, but the sighting was never confirmed.

Since then, more reports have surfaced, suggesting
the Lord God bird may not be gone. A few still hide,

spectral spirits, reminding us of the shimmering line
linking memory and desire, reminding us that perhaps

it's not too late to save them, to save us all.

AFTERWORD

*I don't know whether the bird you're holding
is dead or alive
but I do know it's in your hands.*

Toni Morrison

Since the 1500s, more than 150 bird species around the world have become extinct. In all, one estimate suggests bird losses in the past eight centuries may exceed two thousand species—that's almost one-fifth of all Holocene bird species.[1]

Would we could say we've learned from these extinctions. Instead, scientists suggest that we may well be facing another wave of extinctions exacerbated by climate change. According to a National Audubon Society study based on citizen science conducted over more than a century, more than half the birds studied could be in jeopardy: "Of the 588 species Audubon studied, 314 are likely to find themselves in dire straits by 2080...unless we begin to reduce the severity of global warming and buy birds more time to adapt to the changes coming their way."[2] The report goes on to explain "some bird species will be able to adapt to new climatic conditions, but certainly not all. And while many people assume that climate change will simply shift habitats farther north or to higher elevations...their climatic ranges are not only shifting but also dramatically shrinking. If we stay on our current carbon-spewing path, some of those species may have nowhere to go."[3]

Moreover, climate change isn't affecting only rare species or species on islands, as in the past. Go to the Audubon website and you'll find species listed like the brown pelican, the osprey, the common loon; even our national symbol, the bald eagle, is predicted to lose 73 percent of its breeding range, despite having returned from the brink of extinction once already.[4]

The image of the canary in the coal mine may yet prove to be all too true. We're deep in the coal mine and all around us, not just the canaries are dying. But we must not stop here. On the Audubon website, you can find out how you can get involved.[5]

As poet Toni Morrison reminds us, it's in our hands.

Notes

Preface
The epigraph comes from Katie Ford's poem "To Read of Slaughter," which appears in *Blood Lyrics* (Graywolf Press, 2014).

Passenger Pigeon
To see Audubon's iconic print of the passenger pigeon from *Birds of America*, see *images.library.pitt.edu*.

Great Auk
Great auk specialist John Wolley interviewed the two men who killed the last birds, and Sigurour Ísleifsson described the act.

Labrador Duck
To learn whether the Labrador Duck is extinct, see *macroevolution.net*.

Carolina Parakeet
Since this poem was written, a subspecies of the Carolina parakeet may have been found in the jungles of Peru. For more information, see *cincinnatibirds.com*.

Heath Hen
Artist Todd McGrain made a memorial to the heath hen in Manuel F. Correllus State Forest on Martha's Vineyard: *lostbirdfilm.org*.

Eskimo Curlew
Full details on all sightings up to 1986 are included in the online edition of *Eskimo Curlew: A Vanishing Species?*

Hawaiian O'o
Thanks to Saul Weisberg for his moving poem "Echo," which appears in *Headwaters: Poems and Field Notes* (Pleasure Boat Studio Press, 2015).

Dodo

Thanks to Peter Maas for the information on dodos posted on *The Sixth Extinction* website: *petermaas.nl/extinct*.

Elephant Bird

For more information and to see a video of David Attenborough piecing together the egg of an elephant bird, see *bbc.co.uk/nature*.

Spix's Macaw

Today, the Spix's macaw is declared extinct in the wild, though close to one hundred remain in captivity. Thanks to Tony Juniper for the information chronicled in his book *Spix's Macaw: The Race to Save the World's Rarest Bird*.

Ivory-Billed Woodpecker

For more information on recent sightings and the search for the ivory-billed woodpecker, check the Cornell Lab of Ornithology website: *birds.cornell.edu*.

Afterword

Epigraph: Toni Morrison, *Singing or Silent* exhibit at the Smithsonian, Feb. 2015.

1. Ross MacPhee, afterword "Remember the Islands" from *Swift as a Shadow: Extinct and Endangered Animals* (Boston: Mariner, 1999).

2. Michelle Nijhuis, "A Storm Gathers for North American Birds," *Audubon*, September/October 2014. *audubon.org*.

3. Ibid. "The 188 climate-threatened birds face losing more than half of their current range by 2080, although they have the potential to shift into new areas. The 126 climate-endangered species are projected to lose more than 50 percent of their current range by 2050, with no net gain from range expansion."

4. "The Climate Report," *audubon.org*.

5. "What You Can Do to Help Protect Birds," *climate.audubon.org*.

Further Reading

Albus, Anita. *On Rare Birds*. Translated by Gerald Chapple. Guilford, CT: Lyons Press, 2005, 2011.

Bodsworth, Fred. *The Last of the Curlews*. New York: Dodd, Mead & Company, 1955.

Chilton, Glen. *The Curse of the Labrador Duck: My Obsessive Quest to the Edge of Extinction*. New York: Simon & Schuster, 2009.

Cokinos, Christopher. *Hope is the Thing with Feathers: A Personal Chronicle of Vanished Birds*. New York: Tarcher/Putnam, 2000.

Erhlich, Paul R., David S. Dobkin and Darryl Wheye, eds. *Birds in Jeopardy: The Imperiled and Extinct Birds of the United States and Canada*. Stanford, CA: Stanford University Press, 1992. This book has an extensive bibliography for those wishing to do further reading.

Hollars, B.J. *Flock Together: A Love Affair with Extinct Birds*. Lincoln: University of Nebraska Press, 2017.

Juniper, Tony. *Spix's Macaw: The Race to Save the World's Rarest Bird*. New York: Atria Books/Simon & Shuster, 2002.

Purcell, Rosamond. *Swift as a Shadow: Extinct and Endangered Animals*. Afterword by Ross MacPhee. Boston: Mariner, 1999.

Quammen, David. *The Song of the Dodo: Island Biogeography in an Age of Extinction*. New York: Touchstone/Simon & Shuster, 1996.

Weidensaul, Scott. *The Ghost with Trembling Wings: Science, Wishful Thinking, and the Search for Lost Species*. New York: North Point Press, 2002.

Acknowledgments

I'm grateful to the publishers of the following publications, where these poems previously appeared:

"Passenger Pigeon, *Echtopistes Migratorious*, James J. Audubon, 1824," *The Washington English Journal*, 1997

"Extinct: Laughing Owl, *Sceloglaux albifacies*," *Canary: A Literary Journal of the Environmental Crisis*, Spring 2014

GRATITUDE

First, deep gratitude to Rachel Carson for *Silent Spring* and Fred Bodsworth for *The Last of the Curlews*; reading both books as a child shaped the course of my life, joining my instinctual connection to birds with the knowledge that their continued existence could be in jeopardy.

Gratitude to Robert Michael Pyle for reviewing the manuscript for ornithological accuracy and to Sally Green for her careful reading of the manuscript and many helpful suggestions. Thanks also to Patricia Nerison, Sue Sutherland Hanson, Barbara Brooking, and Tim Cooper for their comments on the preface and afterword.

Myrna Keliher at Expedition Press gave these poems their first home in the form of a beautiful limited-edition letterpress chapbook. It was a thrill to celebrate *Passings'* American Book Award from the Before Columbus Foundation in 2017—and fitting that a small letterpress, itself an endangered art form, would be honored.

Since then, I'm so pleased the birds have found a new home with Jill McCabe Johnson's Wandering Aengus Press. I've valued the opportunity to work with Jill and experience first-hand that she's not only a fine writer but also a skilled editor and book designer. I'm also grateful for the many ways she supports writers and artists in her community.

Speaking of artists, my thanks to Jeff Bessinger, archivist at the Lakeshore Museum Center, for the use of the cover image, "Passenger Pigeons in Flight," and to Jim Ballard for spotting it, and for all his creative suggestions. Thanks to Myrna Keliher for the use of the feather image she designed for the first edition.

As always, I'm ever grateful to my husband, John Pierce, for his support in ways too many to name. Last, a deep bow of gratitude to John's mother, Betty Pierce, who loved all birds and was a steadfast supporter of this book before she passed in 2017, days before the news of the award. This collection is dedicated to her memory.

Poet's Other Books

Hold Fast
Empty Bowl Press, 2020

Passings
Expedition Press, 2016, first edition
Wandering Aengus Press, 2019 second edition
Winner of a 2017 American Book Award

**Contemplative Approaches to Sustainability
in Higher Education: Theory & Practice**
Routledge, 2017

Sailing by Ravens
University of Alaska Press, 2014

The Pen & The Bell: Mindful Writing in a Busy World
Skinner House Press, 2012, co-author with Brenda Miller

Beyond Forgetting: Poetry & Prose about Alzheimer's Disease
Kent State University Press, 2009, editor

Boxing the Compass
Floating Bridge Press, 2007
Winner of the Floating Bridge Press Chapbook Contest

Poet's Habitat and Range

Holly J. Hughes is the author of *Sailing by Ravens* (University of Alaska Press, 2014), co-author of *The Pen and The Bell: Mindful Writing in a Busy World* (Skinner House Books, 2012), and editor of the award-winning anthology, *Beyond Forgetting: Poetry and Prose about Alzheimer's Disease* (Kent State University Press, 2009). Her fine-art chapbook *Passings* (Expedition Press, 2016) received an American Book Award from the Before Columbus Foundation in 2017. A recipient of a Washington State Artist Trust Fellowship and residencies at Hedgebrook, Centrum, Playa, and Artsmith, she taught writing for more than 25 years at Edmonds Community College, where she co-directed the Convergence Writer's Series. She also spent over thirty summers working on the water in Alaska commercial fishing for salmon, skippering a 65-foot schooner and working as a naturalist on ships. She currently serves on the staff of the low-residency MFA program at Pacific Lutheran University, teaches writing and mindfulness workshops, and consults as a writing coach. She divides her time between a home in the Chimacum valley and a small log cabin built in the 30s in Indianola, Washington.

hollyjhughes.com

www.ingramcontent.com/pod-product-compliance
Lightning Source LLC
Chambersburg PA
CBHW062152020426
42334CB00020B/2583